Rougher Yet

Tim Wells lives in Stoke Newington, London, wh ̶ ̶ ̶ ̶ ̶ ̶ ̶ ̶ ̶ ̶ ̶magazine.
He enjoys Chinese food, reggae music and fondly ̶ ̶ ̶ ̶ ̶remembers Harmony,
Symphony, Destiny, Melody and Rhapsody Angel.

Rougher Yet
Tim Wells

Donut Press

Published by Donut Press in 2009.

Donut Press, PO Box 45093,
London, N4 1UZ.
www.donutpress.co.uk

Printed and bound by
The Colourhouse,
Arklow Road Trading Estate, Arklow Road,
London, SE14 6EB.

Donut Press gratefully acknowledges
the support of Arts Council England.

ISBN: 9780955360480

A CIP record for this book is available
from the British Library.

LOTTERY FUNDED

for Angela Mao Ying

Acknowledgements are due to the editors of the following websites and publications in which some of these poems first appeared: www.beatthedust.com, *The Daily Bugle*, *The Delinquent*, *eggsbaconchipsandbeans*, *The Elbow Patch*, *The Fix*, *Fuselit*, *The Illustrated Ape*, *Limelight* (www.thepoem.co.uk), *Litro*, *Lupin*, *Magma*, *Pen Pusher Magazine*, *Penumbra*, *Pox*, *Press 1*, *Reactions*[5] (Pen & Inc, 2005) *The Shuffle Anthology* (Shuffle Press, 2008), *Simper*, *South Bank Poetry*, *Spoonful*, *Straight From the Fridge* (www.upbondageupyours.blogspot.com), *St Vitus Dance*, *The Tally Ho*, *Trespass, The Woofah* and *Yeast*.

Contents

Rougher Yet

When Trousers Give Up the Ghost

One hopes they'll go quietly at home.
You hold them, remember times shared.
A sigh, a moment of introspection,
A strong cuppa, a snifter,
Then back to getting on with it.
Suddenly is worst: the desperation,
Stewart Granger scrabbling
And sinking into quicksand.
The spreading stain in the back of the cab
Reads: *this heist did not go well.*
Rent violently in the High Street –
Shouting your name,
Baring your soul for all the world to see.

Comin' a Dance

In this Dalston dusk
the lights from
the chicken shops,
minicab offices,
Polski Produckti
and all the bling
crammed on the bus
have dazzled the stars.
The sky is a dark sheet
replete with the stains
of an East London
Saturday night.
That stop near
the bottom of The Waste,
a girl dressed as a flapper,
dress cut from twilight,
boards. The feather
in her hair
punches hard times
smack on the nose.
Her bloke's in a pony suit
and drek trainers.
He carries a white fedora –
not even enough
snap to sport it:
a distinct lack of effort.
I hope tonight
she ends up
with someone else.
It's the dark

that makes
the stars shine.
At the next stop
three dancehall queen dem
fresh from Yard,
each wearing less
than she that precedes.
Oh my days!
So much good times
squeezed into
so small space.

When the bass drops …
Lawd G-d Almighty!

Begums

For such tiny teenagers
they sure take up
a lot of the Whitechapel Road.
Some in hairgrips and lip gloss,
some in hijab.
A Smackdown of Sylheti –
Bura bottla! –
a tag team of cockney –
D'ya get me?
The one with the tightest scarf
has the biggest nose.
I wonder if this
is the pressure of the fabric,
an irrepressible act of individuality
forcing its way,
or whether she is just unlucky.

Burger King for a Day

Nasmin is fresh from 'desh less than a year now. Her family are glad she's working, and for the few scraped pounds she wires every month.

Between the breakfast menu and the lunchtime rush she's serving burger and a fucking lot of chips to a sot who's placed a cardboard crown on his head. She turns her head to avoid his breath. He begrudges every penny counted onto the counter, and takes his order to sit with his wallpaper paste bird. 'Oi'm a farking looord!' he bellows. This does little other than cause a couple of kids to start crying, huddling closer to their mums.

Later, at the Job Centre, His Majesty will swear blind drunk he's been looking for work, then burst into tears at the prospect of a job.

Keep the Faith

This smile on my face
Ain't from steering a desk
All workday long.

No, not a 'I'mhappytobeherelikeatwat' smile.
It's knowing that come Saturday night –
Saturday night *all* night –

I'll be with the people America forgot,
Where the fashionable don't go,
Hallelujah!

The boss's stuffed shirt, cufflinks,
Comedy tie and ethical ethics
Won't mean a thing.

They'll all winnow
As Bettye Swann
Starts to sing.

The *thump thump thump*
Up front backbeat
Reducing all to the swagger of generations.

The 4/4 stomp of the week:
'Seven Days Too Long'.
Curtis, Major Lance, Sugar Pie,

In my tenement this poor boy is a king.
The rush of the flush
'Til I come crashing down.

Nine-to-five drudgery,
Pain and heartbreak pounded out
On a powdered killing floor.

Fighting isn't about hitting
It's about getting hit.
This joy in my heart is the best revenge I have.

Playlist

'Make Me Yours' – Bettye Swann
'Seven Days Too Long' – Chuck Wood
'It's All Right' – The Impressions
'You'll Want Me Back' – Major Lance
'Down in the Basement' – Sugar Pie Desanto & Etta James
'In My Tenement' – Roosevelt Grier

Don't Cha Wish Your Girlfriend Was Hot Like Me?

Snow falls. Hands push deeper into pockets.
The girl walking towards me wraps a scarf
tight around herself – the red of her cheeks
a reminder of easier days, the ice beneath
our feet prompting drunken, slurred steps.

My short hair leaves my ears exposed and raw.
Breath wreathes my head. The smell of chicken soup
held longer than its warmth. The crunch of grit,
the maw of winter flexing its jaw to chew
the junkies, the old and the feeble.

It's not too hard on us fat boys.
The hats of the Chassidim set firm.

The Poems of Tibullus

As I start to read this poem
A girl will start coughing,
The pages will skitter
From my hand,
It will dawn on me
It should have been rewritten.

About halfway through,
A mobile will ring,
The ringtone a tune
That sticks in my head,
Round and round and round
'Til the next day
When I go and buy it:
The Sugababes new single.
My girlfriend will laugh at me,
This paining me more than usual
Because I know she is right.

Reaching the end, a heckler
Will think of something to say,
Only this will relate to a comment
Made at the commencement.
I will slur the penultimate line
While the last, if I'm really lucky,
I'll be too drunk to read.

The 1980s are a Long Time Dead

The books in the 'community' bookshop have gathered a lot of dust,
despite being neatly ordered onto Black, Turkish, Lesbian
and Gay shelves. Opposite, Florjan is doing a roaring trade.
Since buying the shop from Mr Choudhury he's added
Polish to the stacks of Caribbean, Turkish, kosher
and English food. The shop is usually busy – busy and noisy.
In the rare moments of calm, Florjan often gazes over
to the faded picture of Maya Angelou in the bookshop window.
He thinks she looks like a nice lady. He wonders who she is,
where she lives, and bets she can put away a lot of salami.

Lay This Burden Down

The Autumn sun is weak
but on my face nonetheless.
In Christ Church Gardens
volunteers are sweeping the leaves,
binning cans
and tidying the beds.
'Look at this,'
a boiler-suited woman says
as she leans on her broom,
reaches down
and lifts a syringe.
'No matter how many
they scatter,
they never grow.'

No. 2 Breakfast

Correction: The Image of the Week on Page 5 of The Knowledge today, purporting to show the artists Gilbert and George looking uncannily like Morecambe and Wise, is in fact of Morecambe and Wise. We apologise for the error.

The Times, July 15th 2006

Gilbert and George are those loveable tosspots who make art of skinheads, shit, spunk, and put their bare bottoms onto stained glass. Oft times they dine in the same caff as me. I love a good caff, the whole history of our country is there: the Dark Ages of black pudding, jam and toast's Tudor robustness, the imperial glory of the fried egg, Industrial baked beans Revolution, Tolpuddle Martyrs mushrooms, the humble banger – 'this was their finest hour' – and the insipid gentrification of the vegetarian option. There's an honesty to these platters. Even when the clock is slow it's telling the right time.

This particular palace, Rossi's, is featured on p. 112 of Russell M. Davies' book *Egg Bacon Chips & Beans*. The entry notes 'the biggest sauce bottles you have ever seen'. Indeed it is a fine establishment: wood, metal-topped tables, cheeky waitresses – all the necessaries. A decent breakfast serves not only body, but nourishes soul and feeds one's character.

One morning, the cook has noticed posters papered opposite for the chaps' latest show, *Was Jasus a Homosexualist?* Not one to be outdone, he prepares and personally serves two steaming plates of the full Monty. Regular punters look on astonished at this hand delivered special – the fried eggs arrayed as eyes, the beans as hair, black pudding nose and the sausages a beaming grin. With the plates laid in front of them, the chaps look down, as deadpan as frying pan, and exchange plates. When George asks Gilbert to pass the brown sauce ... a hush falls.

Karolis Bučinskis

The security guard
where I work
is an officious
young fellow
from Lithuania.
Just yesterday
he'd been outside
enjoying the sun
and eyeing the girls
over the top
of a Stephen King
and was walking
back in as I was exiting.
Being a well dragged up
Englishman
I went to hold
the door open for him.
He, however,
sprinted over,
ran through it,
punched the air,
shouting 'First!'
Not only is there
a breeze of optimism
and opportunity blowing
across the Baltic,
usually he's sat on his arse
drinking far more
coffee than me.

Hypertension

I'm sat with the sphygmomanometer
stilled wrapped round my arm.
I turn the word hypertension
around a few times too.
I tell the doctor I'm amused
that what'll probably kill me
sounds like a camp disco band.
There're still bad romantic decisions
and accidents, I add.
The quack scribbles some more,
without looking up says,
'That's the spirit, son.'

London in Peace

The sunshine slaps my shadow across Hanbury Street.
There's a skip to my step as the latest old song
Grabs me by the ears and snogs me hard;
And London is in loooooove.
The slivers strewn and the sick spewn
Are testament to every rampant lust
That bowl around Hawksmoor's towering prick.
We can touch the sky for but a moment
Before we smack back to the earth of this succulent city.
On the 25, the dippers fleece the crush.
At Shadwell, a knife finds a home.
The art students make neither art nor study.
The phungas do as much nothing as they can.
Today I'll say hello in any one of five languages.
I'll be cursed in English. I'll be blessed by G-d.
The girl who sits behind me in the office
Took the hijab after the last bomb.
She knows now that any moment might be final.
The rumble didn't reach the Vibe Bar.
Who knows when the records will scratch
For the last drink, the last dance,
The last kiss, th

On the Toilet Facilities at Latitude Festival

It doesn't help, reading Ovid's
Metamorphoses on the train;

But once arrived and with tent erected,
Anxiety slips and I start to relax:

Time for a contemplative break.
The toilets are a row of stalls

Set some six foot above a hungry
Chasm. My shit drops and ruins

As fast as the condemned. Paper flutters
Down like prayers. Sat above

This Hades I feel a discernable sense
Of power. Toilets are usually a confining

Affair, bouncing back noise
In cramped confines. Here, the depths

Echo their awful majesty.
Once at the poetry stage I'm to read

After The Scaffold's Roger McGough.
Midway through his set I adjourn

To the backstage Portaloo. As my piss
Arcs perfectly in, I stare down

At the swimming Richards and wonder
Which one is McGough's?

Regimental Museum

The 1914 vintage champagne:
Of course the bottle was empty.
Displayed amidst medals, maps
And cigarette cases that stopped bullets.

When the Germans came across
The cabbage fields it was no picnic.
The bottle passed around.
Did they flinch at the crack of the cork?

Honour and vulgarity toasted as one.
Bravado, hope and fear pulped in the tread.
Tommy Atkins knows a thing or two
About mud and tarts and good times.

Passing the bottle, tasting the moment,
Could all be gone in a pop.
The 1914 vintage champagne:
Of course the bottle was empty.

Weegee

This black and white
crime scene shot
shows the body lying
face down,
arm
      reaching for the gun
just a fingertip away.
A helpful copper
has circled the .38
in chalk.

The girls, the drugs,
the missed opportunities,
laziness and viciousness,
those …
those are all in the shadows.

Funky Broadway

Two black birds are tearing it up.
One has the other by the neck of her lycra top,
strrr-etching it as she backs away.
Licks are raining down, and arms and tits
are swinging wild. At a loud shout –
something uptown I don't understand –
one wraps fingers into her assailant's hair,
and that proud ghetto piece tears away.
It spins across the street, shapes this way
and that, then lands at my feet. I do my best
Roger Moore, stepping coolly over the article.
A kid on a fold-up scooter runs a track through it.

Chelsey Minutes

"If anyone tries to comfort me I will vomit on the balustrade." Chelsey Minnis

We met in a smoothie bar
and talked about
Dark Shadows
and not poetry
for a whole hour.
Her blouse was buttoned
up to the neck.
Her breasts
had the desperation
of two Chinese whores,
faces pressed
to the window
of a burning building.
She was wearing
new shoes
and swung her leg
to show me.
Sensible shoes,
the kind any hot
but coolly dowdy girl
would wear.
When she came back
from the toilet
a square of paper
was stuck
to her heel.
I said
I liked them.

Dance This Mess Around

Early doors,
there's just
the two of us
in the place
and Geri Lynn
serving them up.
Eamon's telling a story –
a Saturday night
got lucky story.
Geri Lynn slams down
two glasses. The beer
rolls 'round
the way the head
of a Jerry Springer
black woman does
just before she sends
a slap to the face
of fool whose hand
is doing all the listenin'.
We sluice a mouthful.
Guys, Geri Lynn asks,
What's the deal
with the finger?
Ya know, sooner or later
when you're with a guy,
it makes its way
back there.
Eamon pauses,
takes stock of the situation
and sagely nods.

He holds up his hand,
unfolds his
index finger
then furls it
into a hook
and poses,
Think of it as a question.

Somewhere,
somebody
is getting them in.

Sunset Park

I meet Brenda Blanco at the corner. I say that if she'd been wearing *un traje rojo* she'd be *Brenda Blanco frum da Bronx*. She ain't. Still, Brenda Blanco from Brooklyn is fine anytime. I'll leave this neighbourhood for Blighty in a few hours. It's a good place: working, mainly Hispanic, people. We're walking for *cawfee*. I laugh at a fried chicken outlet – *Pollo Campano*. The frontage picture of a perky chicken in a fancy hat makes me think of gay cock.
She laughs too, at my pronunciation of *pollo*: Spanish isn't one of my M25 languages. She explains that *campano* means 'from the country'. I tip her the wink.

In the cawfee shop, she orders a slice and I try to get one too. The *heffe* looks puzzled as I ask, and then smiles with recognition as I point. 'I like how you ask for what you want before you point,' she tells me. 'You know he won't understand you.'

'True, but my asking lets him know my manners are good.' My dollars may be crumpled but my nickels and dimes all shine.

Self-Portrait as a PG Tips Chimp

Did Oliver Hardy ever look so good?
I should cocoa! And yes, *Independent on Sunday*,
I'll never scale the same heights as Cheeta
but it's enough to be grafting. D'you know my
Mr Shifter ad', moving the Joanna? That was
top banana – *You hum it son, I'll play it*.
Quality suits (even with the extra-long arms),
ridin' tandem (but not round Hartlepool!),
suppin' me Rosy Lee from a Union Jack mug,
workin' me monkey wrench.
Clock this beatific smile – t'riffic!

The Moon Under Water

Here, pinned to the stained pine,
a halo of barflies:
the locals in comedy hats
making them look like
pints of Guinness;
the darts team presented
with their wooden spoon;
the dead and the faded;
newspaper clippings
where somebody
with the same name
as a regular
did something ridiculous;
a photo of the barmaid
touching the cock
of a statue in Greece –
but hey! That
was a holiday.

Mail Order Bride

He calls her his wife because
he can't pronounce her name.

Men's Lifestyle Choices

Jack London never moisturised.

Real or Fake? Gil Scott Heron
gives you the tell-tale signs.

Erich von Daniken did not know
what to take on a weekend break.

Eddy Merckx knew how to party.

The only thing Max Miller recycled
was other people's jokes.

Hemingway wrote standing up.

Pedicure was a foreign word
to the Tounton Macoutes.

Yukio Mishima did not wear pastels.

Despite dyslexia and an unusually
high voice, General George S. Patton
did not have "issues".

Howlin' Wolf ... down on the killin' floor.

Walking on the Beaches ...

When his workmates ask
how his weekend has been
he'll keep shtum and smile.

The fact was his girlfriend
spent most of it dressing
his cock as Peaches Geldof

then slapping it about 'til
he popped his cork.
She'd waggle his prissied-up prick

in front of her face and yell,
'You're think you're on my guestlist?
You think you're getting into Punk?'

When his cum ran through
her fingers she'd say 'That's it Peaches.
Cry your bitch heart out.'

So, he decides it best to keep quiet,
just smile the smile of the damned.
He spends lunchtime poring

through *Metro*, praying
Peaches hadn't been in a car crash

or got herself stuck in a door ...

Breakfast at Tiffany's

I'm smearing egg yolk over my cafe toast
when two whistled-up golightlys enter,
leave the door ajar, sit at my table.

The cold seeps in. I wrap my hands
round my mug of coffee.

'Peppard says this is a decent caff,' states one.
'How does that facker know?' asks the other.
''E's bin 'ere, ain't he.'

The cat walks out into the rain
and across the path of a black taxi cab.

Wa Do Dem

Back in the early 80s I was a young pisher with a job. All the wedge in my bin went on lager top, windowpane check and Jamdown sound. At the same time, Eek A Mouse was the biggest DJ in the game – not only by virtue of the fact that his choons were massive, but 'cos he stood six-foot-six-inches tall.

One Saturday, music pumping, I was bouncing round my room getting ready to go to one of his shows. I was so excited that I'd forgotten to pull the pins from the new Sherman I'd bought that morning. There I was, stepping round my carpet, blood dripping and Billy Whizzing.

We all met up early doors for a beer by Highbury and Islington tube. Them 2-Tone twins were there with their ghetto blaster blaring Barrington Levy. Later, walking up the Holloway Road, I spotted the Mouse outside the venue with some long-haired berk shoving a microphone in his face. Us skinheads legged it across the road, swerving around sherberts, yelling "Eek A Mouse! Eek A Mouse!" As we drew to the man, the longhair let out a faint "Oh my gawd," in a septic accent. The Mouse looked down at us …

"See it dere! Even de cockney dem a know we!" He stood a further foot taller with the pride.

"Lady, you shot me!"

for Todd Moore on the occasion of his 70th birthday

Sam Cooke's birthday
and everyone is
bringing it on home:
the place swinging
and folks singing.

Skirts haven't been so short
and sayin' so much
since Ike Turner
first kitted out
the Ikettes in St Louis.

At a wink,
a gal in a tasselled dress
camel walks
to a table,
laden with cake.

Ol' Sam snatches up
a handful, rubs it
between her charms,
pushes his grinning face
right on in there:

'Mmmm … THAT'S
the icing on the cake.'
Just then the boys
set the champagne
bottles poppin',

corks ricocheting
off the walls.
Sam blanches,
his attention
on a smear

of heavy strawberry jam
between the girl's
breasts.
Suddenly he feels
cold and alone.

Tanks!

The sodden Somme
September 15th 1916
Stagnant stalemate
At last becomes fluid war
Creeping caterpillars
Popping skulls
Crushing chests
The answer to
German machine guns and wire
Stinking cordite heat
Spewing engine fumes
Crawling charnel house
London's flickering cinemas:
Tanks At The Battle Of The Ancre
Music Hall harlots sing
"We're sure the Kaiser loves
Our dear old tanks"
Ypres generals, whoring troops
Tanks are not expendable, men are
Guns step forward
Again! Again! Again!

Cambrai
November 1917
The Hindenburg Line
Wire so thick you couldn't push
A broomstick through it crushed
To a solid three inch mat
Troops edge forward
Progress!
Further to soaking nemesis
Five mile advance
London's church bells ring
First time since '14
Earl Haig splutters
Machine guns sputter
"A dreadful thing
To put against men …
… Even if they are the enemy"
Progress! Marches on
Followed by the tramp of the lost
To end this slaughter …
Kill! Kill! Kill!

The Language of Pornographic Pictures

One leg raised,
sweat running down
her straining face,
means
she is to be
marked
in this tryst.

Sat upright,
one in each hand,
the press of advancing spears
resembling
the death of Patroclus at Troy:
she will be
run through.

If she be
upon all fours,
firmly rooted,
then she,
my friends,
shall survive
unscathed.

Upon the Occasion of Being Barred from the Rochester Castle Public House

Past midnight and still several miles from N16
When the ginger-haired cunt oirish barman staggers
Onto the 243 bus wherein I am already ensconced.

He teeters onto tiptoes then sprawls into a drop
Sending phone, specs and shekls flying.
I pick up his bins and monotone,
'Can oi have yer gloisses, please?'

I realise now my mistake was in giving them back.
Two days later I walk into the pub
To hear the milkman's kid grizzling, 'Yee're baaaarred.'

Peep Show

Not the gyrations
But the twists that lead here.
Less the proffered pulchritude
More the face-down novel,
Place memorised as she titillates.

The half-eaten sandwich,
High heels on carpet tiles;
Small change comings and goings.
The flaccid conclusion:
Mundanity prevails.

Now the Gate Fly

And what is left
when all this lust
sweats down to nothing?
A love, so subtle.
A love which has reached

its extreme. A love
become immaterial,
become the air
you breathe out
and I breathe in.

The Assassination of Jesse James by the Coward Robert Ford

Back in the day I didn't have a washing machine. Instead I'd take my laundry up Stamford Hill. There was a closer launderette, with a downhill walk, but the woman who handed out the washing powder and did the service washes was psychic. I'd heard her tell about illness, tragedies and heart's secrets many a time. I didn't want her handling my smalls.

So I'd take my bundle up the hill and sit and read the paper as my shirts and trousers sudded and span. The woman there was notable in that she'd wear plastic Safeway bags on her feet, with slippers over them. This was before the coming of Morrisons.

Once I was there waiting on the machine and perusing the paper. A fellow came in to collect his wash. The old woman handed him a neatly folded pile of fresh clothes. He thanked her. She said, 'I found this in your wash ... ' and handed him a gleaming bullet.

He blushed, looked to the floor, palmed it and gave an embarrassed thanks. The film that night was Tyrone Power in *Jesse James*.

Rock Hudson Visits the Most Expensive Whore Buenos Aires has to Offer

Rock emerges from the *salle de bain*
in dressing gown and cravat,
pauses to the plush of the carpet.
The silk of his pyjamas matches
the languor of his eyes.
He pulls the curtains half shut,
running his fingers against the grain
of royal purple velvet.
Lifting a glass of champagne
to the fading evening sun
he looks out across the city –
through the blush of it.
You don't have to act so refined
around me. This is not the Paris Hilton,
she whispers and smoothes the satin sheets.
Her body lying across the bed ruins it for him.
But that's fine, she only wants the money.

Ranting Verse: Delicious Hot, Disgusting Cold

The waitress has just served my breakfast,
And sat facing me
Is a Guardianista Starbucks Arcade Fire tosser
Cutting his sausage *lengthways*.
He dips the slices
Into a perfect circle of red sauce.
The Krzysztof Kieślowski cunt!
I stab mine,
Hack at it in the traditional manner,
Bully the sausage –
A temporary moment
Of triumph in my life
Before the metaphor
Of bubble and squeak
Brings me back to awful clarity.
Job, girls,
Failed ambition, gentrification …
That poor banger copping it all.
Bastard, bastard …
Mmm, beef.
Bastard, bastard …
Mmm, HP
Bastard, bastard …
The waitress smiles at me every day
And how low do I feel
For nearly begrudging that.
Black coffee can be delightfully bitter,
You can always put in miluk.
But no,
It's not me.

There's a twat –
A noo meeja twat –
Cutting his breakfast
Lengthways.
He's probably only in the place
'Cos some trendy scumbag poet
Wrote about Gilbert and George
Breakfasting here.
As I'm choking on my poached egg
And testing the point of the tines
He stands up,
Doesn't take back his plate,
Swings a leather case
By a strap to dangle from his shoulder,
Folds his scarf like an air hostess …

Oh yes,
I should have known.

Come and See

When they were shot it was freezing.
As bullets punched their chests,
steam plumed from the cavities,
blood spattered the snow.

The firing squad were simple folk,
picked precisely for that reason.
As the vapour twisted upwards
one near the centre whispered 'Their souls.'

The officer, a university man,
raised his Shpagin and fired a burst,
shredding the wraiths, sending them
eddying to earth. The sentry pissed his pants.

Smashing Time

It's there on the credits
of NYPD Blue,
just before
the city collapses
to a drum roll.
Marz Bar:
one of the city's finest –
small, narrow, scuzzy.
I stroll in,
order a Heineken,
sit at the bar.
The beer comes cold.
The juke box kicks in
with The Smiths.
A CBGB wannabe
jumps to his feet,
yells 'Turn it up!'

I down my beer
and leave,
sharpish.

Cole Younger, Cold Beer and $ Bills

The story of the crescent-shaped scar
on the cheek and the accompanying
broken nose got better with every retelling.

A stripper was present, for true, but the size
of her bosooms went from there to *there!*
It was the jag of the tooth that first caught the eye.

"We tried a desperate game and lost.
But we are rough men used to rough ways,
and we will abide by the consequences."

Mae Own Mae Clarke

Just to make it stop, he pushed her face
into her lunch – right to the bottom
of her bowl of tepid chicken soup.

She raised up, face dripping stock,
a matzoh ball between her teeth.

When she bit it in half and spat
the remnants across the table,
he knew no good was coming.

A Ruffer Version

That time in Efes, when the killer strolled in, I'm sure Mehmet saw it coming 'cos he blanched, and his eyes moved from the door to the barman, then finally to the man. The gunman walked behind him, still sat in his chair, leant slightly back and then popped him in the head.

I'd thought a skull would burst from a shot, but it was quite the opposite. As Umit said, "There never was much in that head of his."

No explosion, no fountain, no split peach. Just a brief spray of blood. I remember the claret splashing the ear of a girl at the next table. Just that effusive spurt and then a dribble. He slowly leant to one side and settled. I've slept drunk at that self-same table many a time and looked deader.

The quiet was disturbing. Everyone's Thursday night after-hours teetering on a chasm of murder, police and questions, questions, questions.

The assassin held the gun at his side, gave an embarrassed smile and said, "Sorry. So sorry everybody." With that he calmly walked the length of the bar, around the side of the pool tables and was gone into the night.

His calm lingered in the room for a few moments. It was only when a chap knocked over a glass as he fumbled for a drink that the first scream erupted.

Anyway, as I told the Old Bill, I was in the toilet when it happened.

The Empire of the Ants

On his computer *Rome: Total War*
has been running several months.
The Seleucids do his bidding,
and through their might, which
he has carefully crafted, so do
the Egyptians, Macedonians and Greeks.
Already he has laid waste to Pontus,
Armenia and the Parthians. Not even
Crassus managed that. He knows his
growing empire will soon rub with Rome.

At work he is no *diadochus*, no
cataphract, no terror. And those stains
on his trousers … they're just mayonnaise.

Dear Waitress,

Thanks for the smile,
life's curling at the edges
and I only wanted coffee …
It's so good to get just
the smallest peep of sunshine
on this cloudy, frozen morn.

Terms of Employment

We've both been working
in the same office
six years now.

I look at Saly,
Saly looks at me.
Neither of us is happy.

Noel Coward at War

He might be on the conning tower
Or aboard a north Atlantic convoy –
Thick, roll-necked Aran sweater
Or duffle coat toggled against chill winds,
Slung binoculars resting
On his gentlemanly chest,
Eyes steeled to the horizon.
Or a dashing cravat at a country pub;
Leaping from his sports car
To meet the cheery Land Army girl
From the better part of Notting Hill,
telling tales of tailspins
And Messerschmitts.

But wherever he was
This happy breed
Fought war sportingly,
And even though the Luftwaffe
Pounded our Hackney homes to rubble,
As the band stirs faintly
'There'll Always Be an England'
To see toffs and Sirs,
Sleeves rolled up,
Cut chirpy cockney capers
With Tommy Atkins
An' the likes of us,
It makes us proud …
Proud to be British.

Suus Cuique Crepitus Bene Olet

Time and money poured
Through our fingers.
The lager was golden.

We laughed at Prince Buster's boasting,
Hugged to the last rocksteady of the night,
Sang along as Lone Ranger rode the rhythm,

Kept that warmth all through
The night bus journey;
Wrapped it round ourselves,

Slept an innocent sleep,
Buried deep.
Daylight woke us thirsty:

Pull me closer
As I add my call
To the dawn chorus.

Britain's Next Next Top Model

I only have one look
No-one wants to see any bouncing
Designers hate bodies like mine

I look at the camera and I feel it
My job as a model is to be a muse
Put a minger in a frock, call it editorial

English girls, they're supposed to be so street and so cool
I'm a perfect example of what's going on today
I'm so fierce, watch me work the angles

I'd really suit one of those edgy shows
Those bitches, they think they know it all
Watch me work it like a seller

Nine below zero, baby
The self awareness and doubt …
They're really gonna slay me

Ashna's Boyfriend Accompanies Her to Topshop

It's no surprise
this blast
of blistering fashion
melts his cool so fast.
Bright and shiny
fight it out
and Ashna's loyalties flit
from one to the other.
Her attention flies
from this to that
to this to that
to this to 'Oooh!' that.
Between the
nondescript pop songs
X-Ray Spex belt one out.
At this recognition
Ashna gets
even more frantic.
It's at this point
he realises there are
no edges to Topshop,
there is no ending.
The tumble of colour,
cherry prints
and cartoon characters,
is the inside
of her mind
turned out.
He looks as though

he's working out
guitar chords
in his head
but really he's
trying to find
the up escalator.

Steamy Windows

I've been sporting my bins a few months now and they've not steamed up once. This concerns me. I thought I lived a Carry On life, one with a fair dash of sauce, but not once has a peek of cleavage or a peep of arse caused any condensation at all. I feel cheated – by opticians, by circumstance, by life.

In my boyhood it seemed that Charles Hawtrey's fogged like the inside of a Turkish bath every time a winsome young thing bent over. I remark upon this to a bespectacled friend, one who has worn them for years rather than my paltry months. He says that walking into a warm pub from cold weather has done it for him. For several weeks of a 'tatoes spring I've walked into a variety of pubs, East End, West End, even across the river. Lunchtime, afternoon, night … nothing happens. I hunch face down over my usual lager top. I try brandy, whiskey and work my way across the top shelf. Nish. My girlfriend notes my frustration, as she is wont to do. She holds my hand and tells me reassuringly that it'll happen for me. It doesn't. Perhaps I've been looking in the wrong places?

I phone her from work and tell her I'm going to the Olde Axe. That's the best strip pub East London has to offer – best in my parlance being the one where your shoes stick to the carpet, the girls have stretch marks, bruises and it's tears before bedtime – guaranteed.

A couple of hours later, nothing: lager top, arses, salt and vinegar crisps, tits, bad jokes, pussies, a pickled egg and a girl who makes her arsehole wink just inches from my face, which, to be honest, I could have done without. Nothing.

My girlfriend can tell by my boat when I get home that I'm not best pleased, but asks hopefully how it went. I dejectedly shake my head. She tells me that she's sure the former Soviet girls tried their very best for me. She takes both my hands, leans into my face and *haaaaahs* a gentle breath into my face. There! The glasses mist with the fine dew of her whisper. She lifts her index finger and writes her initials onto the lenses – her first upon the left, the last onto the right, in what, to her, must be mirror writing. "What can you see?" she asks.

Oh yes, I love you and you love me.

Sweets

At the table opposite
is sat a Japanese girl
who has just ordered
a *brekkerfast*
and told her friend
she is about to eat
her first sausage.

In the space of a minute,
maybe two,
her face ranges through
curiosity, examination,
recognition, delight
and satisfaction.
It's longer than
I would manage.

Just as she leans
gently forward to swallow,
the menu catches my eye:

Cheery Pie £2.10,
with ice cream £2.20.

It Must be Boring Being Tim Wells

The girls,
the parties,
he's a celebrity … and he got out of there.
The Guardian Review interviewed his dad
and couldn't find an ex
with a bad thing to say.
Seems everything he writes
turns into an Arts Council grant.
O dread prophet!
He walks with Apples and Snakes
and has the ear of the Poetry Society.
The clitterati
throng his readings:
there's not a dry seat in the house.
Has to blakey his brogues
'cos the heels wear down
strolling from book launch
to private view
to premiere.
He'd write even more
if only Scarlett Johanssen
would get off the phone.
He's in everybody's mouth,
held in every hand,
even when a girl says 'no'
there's a poem about it.
Putting the pee into poetry,
if he left a cake out,
it would not rain.

Pam Ayres
ate his words.
How stiff is my vile sense!
Every high brassiered,
low-topped singer
is gonna sing, sing a song,
and superstar DJs admit they were wrong.
In the film of the same name
he'll be played by Ray Winstone,
'cos who's the daddy now?
If I was Tim Wells
I wouldn't have
to waste my time
on pish like this.

There's a Ghost in My House

I remember when fruit juice was served as a starter.

I remember the Corona lorry coming round; limeade was my favourite. I hope all those chemicals caused no lasting damage.

I remember chanukka lights on the menorah atop the Volvos driving around Stamford Hill.

I remember Danny Kendall dying in the back of Bronson's car.

I remember the 253 bus, the 'Yiddish Flyer', when it was a Routemaster. "Fares please!" and hanging onto the pole from the back of the platform, dragging one foot onto the road, sparks streaming up from our blakeys. One time we sped past the Rainbow and yelled abuse at Osmonds fans queuing outside. They chased after us, the bus got stuck in traffic and we had to get off and leg it. Me and me mate never told anyone we were run by girls.

I remember girls practising dance steps in a line at the bus stop.

I remember us all taking sports bags to clubs – each had a towel and talc in it. We'd sprinkle talc on the floor, spin, shuffle, slide, dip and fall back. In the morning my black brogues, red socks and the hems of my blue strides all dusted with white.

I remember my dad not letting gingers into the house in case they soured the food.

I remember herring milt, kidneys and brains on toast: the smell, the texture, the taste.

I remember the *Beano* plopping through the door on an autumn morning and reading it on the sofa with a mug of hot Vimto.

I remember apple doughnuts at Brick Lane on Sunday, blokes on Dodgy Corner with shabby sheepskins, their forearms high with watches.

I remember when football managers dressed like geezers.

I remember "Oh! Ori Ori! Ori Ori Ori Ori Orient!"

I remember antiquing eight-hole Dr Marten boots: melting cherry red polish, brushing, then rubbing black into the creases and buffing 'til they shined. I smelt clean for hours.

I remember twin tubs and my hands red raw from lifting out the steaming wash with wooden tongs.

I remember going to the sea, and my sister and I being scrubbed down outside with white spirit to get all the oil that had spilled ashore off us.

I remember the Cod War and Fisherman's Friends: we had competitions at school as to who could hold the most in their mouth.

I remember sitting on the grass bank outside our class whilst all us lads shouted the theme tune to *The Sweeney*.

I remember when the *Hammer House of Horror* meant an adolescent lad's best chance of eyeing naked ladies.

I remember video nasties. One time we watched *Texas Chainsaw Massacre*. My mate went to the toilet and shit himself at the noise of the washing machine kicking in.

I remember shining pennies and slipping them into the front band of Frank Wright loafers, just behind the tassels.

I remember going to Petticoat Lane to buy Sta-Prest, going out Saturday night, getting drunk on barley wine, kissing a Bank Holiday tart, sleeping on me mate's sofa and them still having a crease come Tuesday.

I remember "Skanga, skanga skanga … Do you believe in love?"

I remember calling fit girls 'lush'.

I remember kung fu films at the flicks, *Broken Oath* with Angela Mao prancing about with a silk scarf. Little did those lecherous villains know it was full of scorpions. Ah ha!

I remember Beardy in *Thundering Mantis*. They kill the teacher AND the kid! He goes berserk, kills the baddies and eats them. Woah!

I remember the Dr Who Museum at Longleat.

I remember holidays visiting the battlefields of England: Bosworth, Maiden Castle and Sedgemoor.

I remember Airfix 1/32 scale soldiers: Afrika Korps, Eighth Army, Ghurkas, German Paratroopers, Commandos.

I remember my girlfriend sewing a $^1/_4$ inch turn-up on my 501s.

I remember, "Remember, remember the 5th of November, gun powder, treason and plot."

I remember history lessons, opening a text book to a picture of the Nuremburg Rally. Some card had drawn a speech bubble so that Hitler was addressing the party faithful with: "und now der UK Subs."

I remember detention. There was no Molly Ringwald, just a gurning, liberal gimp who was wasting his time for my benefit. I made a point of regularly telling him how much I'd enjoyed *The History Man*.

I remember scratchy toilet paper. My grandad used it, even when we'd stopped at school and gone over to the soft stuff. He was a war hero.

I remember the lumps in the school custard.

I remember Mrs Harris' dumplings. If me and Kevin had to work late she'd bring around a big pot of rice 'n' peas 'n' ackee, with salt fish and huge fried dumpling.

I remember pre-release, white label, discomix and slates.

I remember getting a parting razored into my No. 2.

I remember girls with feather cuts and ³/₄ length tonik jackets.

I remember the clothes horse and the airing cupboard.

I remember we called my mum Captain Howdy because we'd hear her creeping about upstairs.

I remember going to the zoo. The rhino was asleep, and scratched onto the hide of its arse in big letters was Tina – my mum's name.

I remember Saturday, the sofa, and a steak and kidney pudding with *World of Sport* wrestling: Cyanide Syd Cooper, Fit Finlay, Mark Rollerball Rocco. The old biddies would bellow, wave their handbags and throw their shoes into the ring. Mick McManus would tear 'em in half and toss 'em back.

I remember thinking that colour was an invention – that all old TV programmes, films and pictures were black and white led me to this conclusion.

I remember the kid down the street's first word: 'bugger'.

I remember our first dog, Topper. Originally he belonged to an old man. Every day my dad would pat him and give him a biscuit on the way to work. When his owner died nobody else could get near him, and they were going to have the dog put down. So my dad brought him home.

I remember goldfish from the rag 'n' bone man.

I remember sending old clothes and blankets to charity.

I remember shrinking crisp packets on the school radiators.

I remember our English teacher telling us we weren't allowed to read Tom Sharpe but he was glad we were.

I remember being too big for the swings and sitting in the rec' reciting 'Sonny's Lettah'.

I remember my grandmother and her golden cans of Special Brew. Us lads drank Old Nick barley wine. It was strong, it was cheap and it had a picture of the Devil on the bottle. The morning after you felt like Jason King looked after a hard night with Ingrid Pitt.

I remember *Babylon*. "Straight from JA to me!"

I remember being flattened by a tidal wave of girls at an Eek A Mouse show.

I remember throwing punches at the 100 Club. It was better than the band.

I remember the Rumble in the Jungle, the heat of that African night stoking the world: "Ali, bomaye!" Ali, the rarest of people – the loudmouth with something to say.

I remember Eddy 'the Cannibal' Merckx.

I remember Derek smashing a plaster statue of the Sacred Heart to pieces with his shoe and then eating them.

I remember painting Airfix kits on the frame, then assembling them and giving them the once over.

I remember the Saturday after payday, wearing a new Ben Sherman to the pub and thinking there must be more to life.

Notes and Queries

Comin' a Dance

This poem takes place on a 67 bus journey between Stoke Newington and Shoreditch.

pony suit: this is not a bloke dressed as an 'orse, though that's possible in Shoreditch, but pony as the rhyming slang for crap (Pony and trap – crap).

drek: Yiddische for crap.

Begums

bura bottla: Sylheti for old fat git. Sylheti is a Bengali dialect commonly spoken around Brick Lane.

Don't Cha Wish Your Girlfriend Was Hot Like Me

The Chassidim are the pious Jews who live on Stamford Hill.

No. 2 Breakfast

Mr George always takes the empty plates back to the counter – the mark of a gentleman.

London in Peace

phungas: Sylheti for bastards.

On the Toilet Facilities at Latitude Festival

Richards: rhyming slang for turds (Richard III – turd).

Wa Do Dem

sherberts: rhyming slang for taxis (Sherbert dab – cab).

Mae Own Mae Clarke

Mae Clarke gets it in the kisser with a grapefruit held by James Cagney in the film *The Public Enemy*.

Steamy Windows

'tatoes: tell a cockney it's a cold day and he or she'll probably say it's 'tatoes. They might even mention having seen a brass monkey rubbing his hands.

nish: nothing.

There's a Ghost in My House

Written after Paul Farley's poem 'I Ran All the Way Home', which was inspired by Joe Brainard's memoir, *I Remember*.

Skanga, skanga, skanga: from the Rupie Edwards single 'Irie Feelings'.

The History Man: The Malcolm Bradbury novel, adapted for TV in 1981.

Captain Howdy: the name given, by Regan, to the demon in *The Exorcist* when it's still scratching about in the attic and answering ouija board questions.

'Sonny's Lettah': a Linton Kwesi Johnson poem from his *Forces of Victory* album.

Babylon: The superb Franco Rosso film about a reggae sound system, released in 1980.

Eddy 'the Cannibal' Merckx: the greatest cyclist, his nickname coming from his drive to win every race.

This book could have been titled:

Achtung – Panzer!, A History of Falling Down, Wicked a Fe Dress Back, Kirkland Laing, Who Feels It Knows It, Wicked Shall Not Reign, We Are the Pigs, Hoping My Sta-Prest Stay Pressed, The Satanic Rites of Tim Wells, Dog War, Trash and Ready, Love A Dub, Right On, Easily Suede, Early Bird Special, Pitching Woo, Keep On Keeping On, I Choked Linda Lovelace, Nicer Than Nice Way, Heavy Makes You Happy, Barry Foster and Other Under-Rated Actors, Make Me Yours, The Answer, For Days and Extra Days, Finest Dancehall Riddims, Undertaker's Burial, I Can Go Anywhere and Still Be Nowhere, Things a Come a Bump, Push In Me Testament, Broader Than Broadway, In Heaven There is No Beer That's Why We Drink it Here, Pie and Mash and Liquor, Never Get Out of the Boat, Discontent, A True Piece of the King, Lord of the Pies, How the West Was Won, Rush Me No Badness, Ain't That Loving You Baby, In a Rub A Dub Style, Cool It Vixen, Nearer My God to Thee, A History of Reggae in Unusual Places, Twice the Lovin' (In Half the Time), Let There Be Version, Kill Them with Version, A Spoonful of Tim Wells, Retort, The Wreck of the Edmund Fitzgerald, Edward II, Bubble and Squeak, Don't You Know Who I Think I Am?, Bunce, Scientist Rids the World of the Evil Curse of the Vampires, Ain't Love Good – Ain't Love Proud, 'Oh … the things I did! The things I did! Oh, the things I did!', Spring Byington, Ranking Slackness, Smashing Time, Champagne Tastes – Lemonade Pockets, 7 Rooms of Gloom, Unrelieved in the Midst of Plenty.

If you enjoyed this book you may also like Jackie Collins' *Dangerous Kiss*.